GET
YOUR
POWER
BACK

GET YOUR POWER BACK

Find and remove the underlying conditions that destroy love and sabotage your life.

BILL FERGUSON

Return to the Heart
P.O. Box 541813
Houston, Texas 77254

www.billferguson.com
www.masteryoflife.com

Return to the Heart
P.O. Box 541813
Houston, Texas 77254
U.S.A.
(713) 520-5370
www.billferguson.com
www.masteryoflife.com

Book design by Mark Gelotte
www.maeric.com

Library of Congress
Control Number: 2007905881

ISBN 1-878410-41-5

Printed in the United States of America

This book is dedicated to Sue: my wife,
my partner and my best friend.

INTRODUCTION

If you have a relationship, or any other area of life that isn't working, there will always be an underlying condition of resisting or hanging on that is creating the problem.

This condition creates a state of fear, upset and tunnel vision that takes away your power. It keeps you from finding solutions and forces you to act in a way that actually makes your situation more difficult.

This underlying condition is created by certain specific core issues from your past. Until these issues are healed and the condition removed, you will be powerless in this area of your life. The problem area will continue, and you will be forced to repeat the past.

The first part of this book shows how we create our lives, particularly the areas of life that don't work. Once you discover why your life is the way that it is, you become more able to determine how your life will be.

The second part of the book is about finding and actually removing the specific underlying conditions that sabotage your life. As you do this, the problem areas of your life begin to clear up.

Instead of creating a life of fear and upset, you create a life of love and opportunity. You restore the happiness and freedom you once had. You become far more effective and much more able to have your dreams come true.

At the end of each chapter, there will be a page that suggests specific action to take. Take the action and watch for miracles.

PART I

WHY CERTAIN AREAS OF LIFE DON'T WORK

PART II

BE FREE OF THE UNDERLYING CONDITIONS THAT SABOTAGE LIFE

PART I

WHY CERTAIN AREAS OF LIFE DON'T WORK

CHAPTER 1

We Create Our Lives

We create our lives. We create our lives out of the way we see life. We then act consistent with the way we see life and life responds accordingly.

This is why each person's life is so different. The type of situations and circumstances that show up in one person's life are totally different from those that show up in the next person's life.

Notice that there are certain areas of your life that work effortlessly. These same areas will be disaster zones for someone else.

Now notice that there are certain areas of your life where you suffer. These areas may clear up from time to time, but they keep coming back. They keep coming back because you keep creating them.

The type of situations that show up in your

life are a reflection of how you relate to life. When you change how you relate to life, you change what gets reflected back.

When an area of life isn't working, we think that the problem is the result of our circumstances, but this is an illusion. The circumstances are not the problem. They are the symptom of something much deeper. The real problem is an underlying condition of resisting or hanging on.

This condition creates a state of fear, upset, and tunnel vision that destroys your ability to see clearly. It keeps you from seeing what needs to be done, and forces you to act in a way that either creates the problem or keeps you from resolving it.

Every time a relationship or any other area of life isn't working, this condition will be present.

Until this underlying condition is found and removed, you will be forced to act in the same way, which will produce the same result. The problem will continue and your life will remain the same.

If you want to resolve a problem area of your life, take your focus off of the symptoms, and put your focus on finding and removing the condition that creates the problem.

The moment you do this, everything changes. You restore your peace of mind and see your situation in a very different way. Solutions appear and this area of life starts clearing up.

Fortunately, the process for finding and removing this condition is very simple and very fast. This book will walk you through the steps.

Throughout this book, you will discover certain profound truths. As you let in these truths, they will change the way you live your life. This in turn changes what happens in the world around you.

Let's start the process by looking at the law of cause and effect.

The law of cause and effect

"Cause and effect" is the relationship between two events. For example, if your telephone rings, you will probably answer it. The telephone ring is the "cause" and your answering it is the "effect." The "cause" produces the "effect."

At any moment, you are totally, 100% at the effect of the world around you. No matter what happens around you, you will react accordingly.

At the same time, the world around you is totally 100% at the effect of you. Whatever you do, or don't do, the world around you will react to you. This makes you the cause.

You are totally at the effect of everything around you. You are also the cause. You are both at the same time. You react to the world around you and the world reacts to you.

Although you are both, you only experience yourself as being one or the other. You either experience yourself as being the "cause" of your life or you experience yourself as being "at the effect."

How you experience yourself at any moment determines both the quality of your life and what happens in it.

When you experience yourself as being "at the effect," you are the victim of your circumstances and you have no power. Your confidence quickly drops. You close down, become negative, and lose your ability to take effective action.

Every time you are upset and every time you are faced with an area of your life that isn't working, you are "at the effect."

Think of a time when you have been in this

state and notice how uncomfortable it was.

Now find a time when you were "at the effect" of something and for some reason, you decided that you had had enough. You reached your limit and decided to take action. You then took steps to turn your situation around.

Notice how you felt when this happened. Instantly, you got your power back. You felt good about yourself and good about life. You became confident, creative, and full of energy.

Instead of the circumstances having power over you, you gained power over your circumstances. Without knowing, you shifted from being "at the effect" to being "at cause." You changed your life and you did it with nothing more than a thought.

When you live your life "at cause," you have power over your life. You are on top of your circumstances. You can chart your course and you can make your dreams come true.

When you are "at the effect," you feel like your circumstances are on top of you. You are powerless and unable to move forward.

In this book, you will learn what puts you "at the effect" and how to live "at cause." You will learn why certain areas of your life don't work and how to have them clear up. You will learn the key to creating a life that will exceed your dreams.

Action To Take

1. Notice that there are certain areas of your life that consistently don't work. These problem areas may clear up from time to time, but they keep coming back. Make a list of the specific areas of life where you suffer.

2. Any area of your life that isn't working is an area where you are "at the effect." Instead of you having power over your circumstances, your circumstances have power over you. Look over the items on your list and see that this is true.

3. Notice how powerless you feel when you are "at the effect." What happens to your confidence and your level of happiness? How does it feel when you are "at the effect?"

4. Find a time when you shifted from being "at the effect" to being "at cause." How did you feel after you made the shift? What happened to your confidence, your effectiveness, and your level of happiness?

5. Imagine what your life would be like if you lived "at cause" most of the time. What would happen to the quality of your life and your ability to have your dreams come true? Take a few moments and notice how different your life would be.

CHAPTER 2

The Happiness That We Seek

Ultimately, the happiness that we seek is something called "the experience of love." When you are in this state, you automatically interact in a way that has life work.

To see this in your life, look at what happens in you when you feel loved and appreciated. You are happy, alive and free. You feel good about yourself and good about your life. You are confident and creative. You see life clearly and are very effective.

You also have a very positive attitude. You radiate this positive energy into the world around you and life reflects it back. Great things happen when the experience of love is present.

Take a moment now and notice how you feel when you are in this state. Isn't this the happiness that you seek? Isn't this what you want in your relationships and in your life?

Now notice where this state is located. Is it outside of you or inside of you? Obviously, it's inside of you. The experience of love is an inner state.

The opposite state is one of fear and upset. When you are in this state, life is painful. You close down and lose your ability to see clearly. You also become very negative. You become negative in your thinking, your speaking, and in your actions.

You then radiate this negative energy into your life and life gives it right back. Without knowing, you create opposition and resistance against yourself. Negative things happen all around you.

Notice how if feels when you are in this state. Now notice where the feelings are located. They are not in your circumstances. They are inside of you.

Fear, upsets, and the experience of love are all states of mind. One moment you feel one way and in the next moment you feel another way. Sometimes you are in the experience of love and sometimes you are in a state of fear and upset.

The particular state that you are in at any moment seems to be the result of what happens around you, but as we'll soon see, this is an illusion. Your state of mind is not determined by what happens. It's determined by how you relate to what happens.

Instead of your circumstances determining your inner state, your inner state determines what kind of circumstances show up in your life.

When you are in the experience of love, you radiate a positive energy and great things happen. When you are full of fear and upset, you radiate a negative energy and painful things happen.

Your inner state determines how you relate to life, which determines how life responds to you. But this is not what we have been taught. We have been taught that happiness and upsets come from outside of us.

As long as we believe that happiness and upsets come from outside of us, we will go through life trying to force our circumstances to be a certain way.

For example, if I think that happiness comes from my wife treating me a certain way, then I have to do whatever I can to make her treat me this way.

The problem with this way of thinking is that

the more we try to force people and life to be a certain way, the more we create the exact opposite of what we want.

Instead of creating the happiness that we seek, we create more fear and upset. We destroy the experience of love. We sabotage our lives and keep our dreams from coming true.

A good way to see this is to look at the law of resistance.

The law of resistance

One of the most powerful ways that we sabotage our lives is by resisting. When we resist, we magnify and give power to whatever we are resisting. Here are some examples that demonstrate this:

Imagine four yellow balloons on the ceiling above you. Now, whatever you do, don't think of them. You just thought about them. Don't do that.

What happens when you fight the yellow balloons? You keep thinking about them. In fact, you can hardly think of anything else. Resisting the thought of yellow balloons gives the thought power and keeps it alive.

The same principle applies to every aspect

of life. Whatever you resist gets magnified.

Have you ever had a relationship with someone who had a characteristic that you couldn't stand? What happened to that characteristic when you resisted it? It grew. It grew in your perception and it actually showed up more around you.

Let's say that you are married and that you are resisting losing your spouse. The more you resist losing your spouse, the more you hang on, and the more you push your spouse away.

Look at how you feel when someone resists the way you are and tries to change you. How do you feel about changing? You don't want to. You get upset and become resistant. You don't want to change a thing.

The same thing happens when you resist someone else or any other aspect of your life. The very act of resisting makes whatever you resist more solid.

Let's look at fears. A fear is created by resisting a future event. If I have a fear of losing someone, I am resisting the future event called losing the person.

The more I resist losing the person, the bigger my fear. The bigger my fear, the more I feel threatened and the more I hang on. The more I hang on, the more I push the person away, which brings me my fear.

Notice that whatever you fear and resist keeps showing up in your life. By resisting, you create the very circumstances that you are avoiding.

Look at any area of your life that doesn't work. This will be an area of life where you are resisting. Now look at any area of your life that works great. This will be an area where you can flow with whatever happens.

Fighting and resisting an aspect of life does not make it go away. Resisting gives it more power.

Action To Take

1. Find a time in your life when you felt loved and appreciated. Notice how good you felt. You were happy and alive. You radiated a very positive energy and great things happened around you. Isn't this the happiness that you seek?

2. Notice how positive you are when you are in the experience of love and how negative you are when you are in a state of fear and upset. Notice how your attitude determines what action you take.

3. The world responds to whatever state you are in. When you radiate a positive energy, great things happen around you. When you radiate a negative energy, negative things happen. Notice how your attitude determines what happens in your life.

4. Notice that the areas of your life that work great are areas where you can flow with whatever happens. The areas of life that don't work are areas where you fight and resist.

5. By resisting, you magnify and give power to whatever you are resisting. Look in your life and find examples of the law of resistance.

CHAPTER 3

The Nature of Upsets

At any moment, your life is exactly the way that it is. The people in your life are the way that they are, you are the way that you are, and the circumstances of your life are the way that they are.

Everything may change tomorrow, but at any moment, your life is exactly the way that it is. Look in your life and see how true this is. Notice how totally irrelevant your feelings are about this.

When you are at peace with the truth of the way your situation is, you have peace of mind. You see your situation clearly and can see what needs to be done. Solutions appear and you become very effective.

When you fight and resist the truth of the way things are, you make everything worse. You create a state of fear, upset, and tunnel vision.

You lose your ability to see clearly and you interact in a way that magnifies the problem.

Upsets may seem to be caused by what happens, but they're not. Upsets are caused by fighting and resisting what happens.

To see this in your life, select a recent upset. Now notice what would happen to the upset if, somehow, you were at peace with what happened. There would be no upset.

There would be no upset because the upset wasn't caused by what happened. The upset was caused by fighting and resisting what happened.

The moment you take away the fighting and resisting, the upset disappears. You restore both your peace of mind and your effectiveness.

Now notice what would happen if someone spilled a glass of water on you. You would be wet, and you would be wet whether you liked it or not.

Your being wet is like any other circumstance in life. It's something that happens outside of you and your feelings about it are irrelevant.

Upsets, on the other hand, are located inside of you. Since an upset is something that happens on the inside, there has to be something on the inside that creates it.

We create our upsets by fighting and resisting what happens.

Let's go back to the water. If you were at peace with being wet, there would be no upset. If you fought being wet, you would be upset, and the more you fought it, the more upset you would be.

The upset has nothing to do with being wet. The upset can only exist if you are fighting being wet. The same is true with all the circumstances of your life. Nothing has the power to create an upset in you. Only you can do that.

Take a moment and let this in.

Knowing that you are the source of your upsets is one of the keys to getting your power back. This is important because of all the damage that upsets generate.

When we get upset, we close down inside. We become so full of emotion that we lose our ability to see clearly. We also get tunnel vision.

We get tunnel vision because our circumstances are striking a nerve. Subconsciously, we feel like our survival is being threatened.

In an automatic, subconscious attempt to protect ourselves, we put all our focus on resisting the perceived threat. This narrow focus then creates a state of tunnel vision that quickly makes any situation worse.

This tunnel vision sabotages our lives in two very specific ways:

1. It destroys our ability to discover solutions. We can't find the solutions because they are outside of the tunnel vision.

2. It forces us to fight and resist the perceived threat, which then magnifies the problem.

Here is an example:

Robert was married and had a fear of losing his wife. In a subconscious attempt to make sure she didn't leave, he hung on to her. He tried to control her and did everything he could to make sure he didn't lose her.

Robert was so focused on making sure she didn't leave, he acted in a way that pushed her away. Instead of creating an environment where his wife would enjoy being with him, he created an environment where she wanted to avoid him.

This result was exactly opposite of what he wanted, but this is the nature of tunnel vision.

Instead of creating what we want, it brings us the opposite.

If Robert had given his wife the freedom to be the way she was and to chart her own course in life, she would have felt empowered instead of suppressed.

This probably would have saved his marriage, but doing something like this would have been impossible for Robert. It would have been outside his tunnel vision.

Any area of your life that isn't working is an area where this tunnel vision is present. By fighting your circumstances, you destroy your ability to see clearly. You give your situation power and keep it from clearing up.

Resisting puts you "at the effect."

Do you remember our discussion about cause and effect? When you are "at the effect," you are the victim of your circumstances. You have no power. Confidence and effectiveness disappear.

When you are "at cause," you are on top of your situation. You have power and can chart your course. You have peace of mind and can see what needs to be done. You can take effective action.

Being at the effect is a painful state. It's also something that we create. We put ourselves at the effect by fighting and resisting the truth of the way our circumstances are.

When this happens, you give your power to whatever or whoever you are resisting. Instantly, you put yourself "at the effect." You become a victim of your circumstances and you become very ineffective.

Look at any area of your life that isn't working. Notice that there are certain circumstances that are present – and you are fighting them. For example: your spouse wants to leave or you don't have enough money to pay the bills.

The more you fight and resist these circumstances, the more you put yourself "at the effect." You get upset, lose your ability to see clearly, and magnify the problem.

If you could surrender to the truth of what's so, the fear, upset, and tunnel vision would disappear. You would see your situation clearly and could see what needs to be done. You would restore your effectiveness and this area of life would clear up.

So why can't we be at peace with the truth of the way our circumstances are?

We fight our circumstances because they trigger a suppressed hurt from the past. To say this another way, the circumstances strike a nerve.

This is why different people get upset at different things. Each person has a different set of nerves, or core issues, that get triggered.

This is also why the same type of upsets and the same self-sabotaging behavior patterns keep showing up in your life. The same situations keep showing up because the same nerve keeps getting struck.

It's the subconscious avoidance of this hurt that sabotages your life. Every area of your life that doesn't work can be traced to this hurt.

Finding and healing this hurt is one of the most important things you can ever do.

Action To Take

1. Make a list of at least twelve times when you have been upset. List the times that you have been angry or hurt. List every major upset that you have had in your life.

2. Then for each incident, notice what would happen to the upset if you were totally at peace with what happened. There would be no upset. Work with this until it is obvious that upsets are not caused by what happens.

3. Look over your list and notice that the same type of upset keeps showing up in your life. The same type of upset keeps showing up because the same suppressed hurt keeps getting reactivated.

4. Locate the hurt that is under each upset. Notice that this is an emotion that you would do almost anything to avoid feeling.

5. Now notice what happens to your effectiveness when you get upset. What happens to your ability to see clearly? Don't you get tunnel vision? Notice how the tunnel vision destroys your ability to find solutions and makes your situation worse.

CHAPTER 4

The Hurt That Sabotages Our Lives

When you were a young child, you were pure love. You were happy, alive and free. But you were born into a world that suppresses this state. As a result, you got hurt, and you got hurt a lot.

As a little child, the only way you could explain these painful losses of love was to blame yourself. In a moment of hurt, you created the belief that you were worthless, not good enough, a failure, not worth loving, or in some other way, not okay.

This wasn't the truth, but to a little child, this was the only explanation that made any sense at the time. You then fought the very notion that you created. "No one can ever love me if I'm worthless. Worthless is a horrible way to be."

The moment you decided that you were not okay, you created a mechanism, or core issue, that would then sabotage the rest of your life. From that moment on, the underlying focus of your life would be to avoid this hurt.

Here is an example of how this hurt gets created.

Several years ago, I was shopping in a local department store when I saw a mother yelling at her little four-year-old daughter. Apparently the little girl had spilled her drink and the mother was quite embarrassed.

"What's the matter with you?" the mother yelled. "Why are you so stupid?"

The mother was so loud and hateful that everyone stopped and stared. The little girl was devastated. She experienced a very painful loss of love and started crying.

Imagine what this must have been like for the little girl. This would have been extremely painful.

Then she did something that would change the rest of her life. She created the belief that she was stupid.

This wasn't the truth, but to a young girl in a moment of deep hurt, this became her truth. What else could she conclude?

"My mom knows everything, and she says I'm stupid. Clearly this must be true. Besides, I did spill my drink and yesterday I got my shoes muddy."

The little girl couldn't help but believe that she was stupid. This is especially true if her mother tells her this over and over.

The girl started out being free and alive – full of love and joy. Then she discovered that something was terribly wrong with her. She was stupid. The hurt of this realization would have been unbearable.

Then the little girl took the process one step further. She started fighting the very belief that she created.

"No one can ever love someone who's stupid. Look at my mom. Even my mom doesn't love me because I'm stupid. Stupid is a horrible way to be. I can't be stupid. I have to be smart. If I really am stupid, I shouldn't even be alive."

The little girl will then spend the entire rest of her life running from the suppressed hurt of feeling stupid, doing everything she can to become smart.

Have you ever known someone who has to be right or who acts like they know it all? This is someone who is running from the hurt of feeling stupid. This person will also be unable to receive criticism and will have a major fear of making a mistake. The result is more mistakes and more hurt.

The same thing happens to every one of us. Each person has a different hurt and each person avoids it in a different way, but the result is always the same. The areas of life affected by our hurt will be full of suffering and struggle.

Here are two examples of how these core issues sabotage our lives.

Example 1

When Rhonda was growing up, her father was so occupied with his work that he seldom paid any attention to her. When he did pay attention, he would yell at her. She felt totally unloved.

As a result, Rhonda couldn't help but create the belief that she wasn't worth loving. This wasn't the truth, but it became her truth. She would then spend the rest of her life running from this hurt.

In an automatic attempt to avoid this hurt, she created a state of tunnel vision that would then sabotage all her relationships. Instead of looking for what works, her focus would be on trying to control life and force people to treat her a certain way.

Whenever something happened that triggered her hurt, Rhonda became full of fear and upset. She would then get angry and be hurtful.

No matter how hard the men in her life tried, they could never treat Rhonda in a way that made her happy. She would constantly get upset about one thing or another.

She would also hang on to the men in her life. She had to, because if someone left, this would trigger all her hurt. To avoid this hurt, she hung on.

Rhonda was so hard to live with, she pushed everyone away. Without realizing it, she kept creating more and more of the very hurt that she tried so desperately to avoid.

Example 2

No matter what Mark did, it was never enough to get his father's approval. As a result, he created the belief that he was a failure. He then spent the rest of his life running from this hurt, doing everything he could to become a success.

In his attempt to avoid the hurt of failure,

he would overspend. He would do everything he could to have a higher standard of living so that he could feel like a success.

In his attempt to feel like a success, his debt got bigger and bigger. Eventually, he had trouble paying the bills and failure was in his face like never before.

This was very threatening to Mark. He then became so full of fear and upset that he lost his effectiveness at work. Then his income dropped and his situation got worse. This magnified the fear and made him even more ineffective.

Mark eventually worked his way out of the problem, but the need to be a success continued and the same type of situations kept showing up in his life.

By Mark's running from failure, he created a life full of failure.

What are the areas of your life that don't work? Where do you suffer?

Any relationship and any area of your life that doesn't work is an area where a specific suppressed hurt from the past, or core issue, is being triggered.

In an automatic, subconscious attempt to avoid this hurt, you create a state of fear, upset, and tunnel vision. You lose your ability to see clearly and you act in a way that literally creates more hurt.

Find the areas of your life that don't work and look for the underlying tunnel vision. Notice how this tunnel vision keeps you from discovering solutions and forces you to act in a way that magnifies the problem.

Later in this book, you will learn how to heal your hurt, remove the tunnel vision, and have the problem areas of your life clear up.

Action To Take

1. Go back in time and put yourself in the hurt that you experienced as a child. Then see if you can identify it. In the eyes of a little child, what would those painful circumstances say about you?

2. How would it feel if you really were worthless, not worth loving, not good enough, or whatever your hurt is? Notice how painful this would be. Notice how much you have avoided this hurt.

3. When this hurt gets triggered, you become full of fear and upset. You get tunnel vision and tend to make your situation worse. Look at your life and see how the automatic avoidance of this hurt has sabotaged your life.

4. Now go to your list of upsets and see if you can find the hurt that is under each upset. Find the specific words of "not okay" that most accurately describe this hurt. Notice that the same hurt keeps showing up in your life, over and over again.

5. The truth and the hurt have absolutely nothing to do with each other. To say that you really are this way would be nonsense. It's not the truth, but it is the hurt. Make sure you see the difference.

CHAPTER 5

How We Create and Destroy Love

To see the consequences of resisting from a different perspective, let's look at the nature of love and relationships.

Love by itself is never enough to have a relationship work. The divorce courts are full of people who love each other. For example, what good is someone's love for you if the person treats you poorly?

To have a relationship be great, you need more than love. You need the experience of love. If I want my relationship with you to be great, I need to make sure you feel loved.

When the experience of love is present, you are happy and alive. You feel good about yourself. You are positive, confident, and creative.

Ultimately, this is the happiness that we seek. This is what we want in our relationships and in our lives. So what creates the experience of love?

It's created by giving acceptance and appreciation.

Notice how you feel when someone genuinely accepts and appreciates you. Doesn't this feel good? Of course it does. You feel empowered. You feel better about yourself and better about life.

You also feel better about the other person. Without thinking, you automatically become more accepting and appreciative of the person who accepts you.

The same thing happens when you accept and appreciate someone else. That person feels better about life and better about you. Then you feel better about the other person. Then the other person feels better about you.

You soon create a cycle of loving, supporting, and empowering each other. This cycle of love brings out the best in people and creates the happiness that we seek in our relationships.

By giving acceptance and appreciation, you create the experience of love, and great things happen.

This is the way most romantic relationships

begin. They start out great, but they seldom stay this way. This is because sooner or later, someone's hurt from the past gets triggered.

When this happens, the person feels threatened. In an attempt to avoid feeling this hurt, the person puts up his or her walls of protection.

Then the person becomes judgmental, critical and otherwise non-accepting. It's this non-acceptance that destroys the experience of love.

Notice how you feel when someone is judgmental and critical towards you. Instantly, the experience of love disappears. You get hurt and upset. You put up your walls of protection and automatically resist the person who is non-accepting toward you.

The same thing happens when you are non-accepting, judgmental or critical towards someone else.

That person gets upset, puts up his or her walls of protection, and becomes more judgmental and critical towards you. Then you get more upset at the other person. Then the other person gets more upset at you.

Without knowing, you create a cycle of conflict, a cycle of hurting, attacking and withdrawing from each other. This cycle then goes on and on without either person ever noticing his or her role in the problem.

It's this cycle of conflict that creates the suffering in relationships.

By resisting the way someone is, you destroy the experience of love. You then create opposition and resistance against yourself. To end the cycle of conflict, or to make sure it never starts, stop the resisting.

The cycle of conflict is like a tennis volley. It takes two people to keep the volley going, but only one to end it. As soon as someone refuses to return the serve, the volley is over.

To end the cycle of conflict, stop fueling the fire. Accept the person the way he or she is. This is the key to having any relationship work.

Unfortunately, this is much easier said than done. Some people are very difficult to accept.

Fortunately, acceptance is nothing more than surrendering to the truth. The people in your life are exactly the way that they are whether you like it or not.

Pick someone in your life that you can't accept. Notice that this person has a very particular state of mind and a very particular way of seeing life. Notice that this person is exactly the way he or she is and that your feelings about it are totally irrelevant.

When you are at peace with the truth of the way someone is, you have peace of mind and can see your situation clearly.

You may discover that the person isn't for you. Maybe you need to move on. Maybe you need to do something else. By being at peace with the truth, you can see what you need to do.

When you fight the truth, you create a state of fear, upset, and tunnel vision. This destroys your ability to see clearly and forces you to fight, resist, hang on, or withdraw.

This in turn destroys the experience of love, fuels the cycle of conflict, and makes your life more difficult. By fighting the truth of the way someone is, you literally create more suffering.

The biggest killer of relationships is not being at peace with the truth of the way the other person is.

To learn more about how to end the cycle of conflict, read my other book, *How To Heal A Painful Relationship.*

Whether you resist the way someone is or you resist a specific area of your life, the result is always the same. You magnify the problem and make your life more difficult.

Action To Take

1. How does it feel when someone genuinely accepts and appreciates you just the way you are? Doesn't this feel great? Notice how happy and positive you become. Noticc how you treat this person in return.

2. Now notice how you feel when somconc is judgmental or critical towards you. Notice how you respond. The same thing happens when you are judgmental or critical towards someone else. That person gets hurt, puts up his or her walls of protection, and gives it back to you. Let this in.

3. The same principle applies in every aspect of life. Any area of your life that isn't working is area where you are resisting. By your resisting, you create opposition and resistance against yourself. Find some examples of this in your life.

4. Make a list of every relationship you have that isn't working. Notice that you have been fighting the truth of the way these people are. Notice how your resisting has destroyed the experience of love and fueled the conflict.

5. Whenever there is a cycle of conflict, there must be two people participating. Look at any relationship you have where there is conflict and see your role in the problem.

CHAPTER 6

Accepting 100% Responsibility

Once you discover your role in a particular problem, you can turn your situation around.

When you can't see your role in the problem, or when you blame someone else or some circumstance for your situation, you put yourself "at the effect." You lose your power and you stay stuck.

To see how this works, let's take another look at relationships.

We have been taught that relationships are 50/50, but they're not. They are 100/100. Each person is 100% responsible for the presence or absence of love.

Let's say that you and I have a relationship. How I treat you determines how you will treat me. If I am loving and supportive, you will react one way. If I am judgmental, critical, or controlling, you will react in quite a different way.

This makes me 100% responsible for the presence or absence of love, and you are 0% responsible. You are 0% responsible because no matter what I do, you will respond accordingly. I'm the cause and you are the effect.

The other side of the coin is also true. How you treat me determines how I react to you. You are the cause and I am the effect.

If you are loving and supportive, I will react one way. If you are judgmental, critical, or controlling, I will respond in quite another way. This makes you 100% responsible.

Both of us are totally, 100% responsible for the presence or absence of love, but this is not what we have been taught.

We have been taught that there is only one responsibility. Either you are responsible or I am responsible, or we cut it down the middle, 50/50.

This is what we've been taught, but it's not the truth. Everyone is responsible. When we believe that there is only one responsibility, we get into serious trouble. Here's why:

Let's say that you and I have a problem in

our relationship. Since I know that there is only one responsibility, it's easy to find the source of the problem. It's you.

Then I get trapped. I get trapped because when I point at your 100%, I'm telling the truth. You are responsible. And since I have found the source of the problem, I don't have to look any further.

The problem with this is that whenever I blame you, I give you all my power. When I point at your 100%, I'm saying that I'm 0% responsible, and if I am 0% responsible, I have zero power.

"There is nothing I can do about the situation. You're the problem, not me."

As long as I focus on your 100% responsibility, I can't see mine. When I can't see my 100%, I can't see what needs to be done. This keeps me stuck.

Whenever you blame someone, you may be telling the truth, but you are also making yourself a victim. To get your power back, stop blaming and find your role in the problem.

If you are in a cycle of conflict, notice that you have been fighting the truth of the way that person is. Notice that you did not make sure that the other person felt loved, accepted and appreciated. Notice that you have been judgmental, critical, and perhaps controlling or hanging on.

Notice that the other person got hurt, put up his or her walls of protection, and gave it right back to you. Then you got upset and became more critical of the other person. Then the other person got more upset at you.

Notice that you single-handedly destroyed the love and fueled the conflict in your relationship.

This is not a fun thing to see, but it's the key to getting your power back. It's also the key to ending the cycle of conflict. You may need to stretch to see your 100%, but it will be well worth your effort.

So, why do we blame? The whole purpose of blaming is to take the focus off of ourselves. "You are the problem, not me." I blame you so I don't have to look at myself. I don't want to see my role in the problem.

More specifically, I don't want to see that I am the problem. I don't want to see that my situation is the way that it is because I am worthless, not worth loving, a failure, or some other core issue.

It's not the truth that we are this way. It's just a suppressed hurt. But it's a hurt that we will do almost anything to avoid feeling. So, in a subconscious attempt to avoid this hurt, we blame. We then lose our power and become totally ineffective.

Life only works in the areas where we take responsibility for the result. When you blame, you can't take responsibility. When you can't take responsibility for the result, you can't take effective action, and the problem will continue.

Sometimes our role may be as little as staying in a destructive environment. Usually our role is much more, but one thing is for sure if you have an area of your life that isn't working, you have something to do with it.

You are either resisting the truth of the way your situation is or you are resisting how your situation may become. Either way, you create a state of fear, upset, and tunnel vision that takes away your power, magnifies the problem, and prevents you from finding solutions.

Any area of your life that isn't working is an area where you are resisting. Let go of the resisting, and this area of life will start clearing up.

Action To Take

1. Relationships are not 50/50. They are 100/100. Get your list of difficult relationships and find your 100% responsibility for the loss of love in each relationship.

2. Remember that the other person is also 100% responsible, but pointing at that person doesn't do you any good. It makes you a victim and takes away your power.

3. Once you see your role in a problem, you can do something about it. When you blame, you give your power away. You get tunnel vision and lose your ability to take effective action. Let this in.

4. We blame in an automatic attempt to avoid feeling some hurt. Make a list of the areas of life where you blame. Then find the hurt that you are avoiding. What painful thing would it say about you if you were the problem?

5. Now make a list of every area of your life that isn't working. Then notice that for each item on your list, you have something to do with it. When you focus on your role in the problem, you become very effective.

CHAPTER 7

We Fight the Truth

My wife and I have a black and white cat. No matter how much I want that cat to bark, it isn't going to. I can yell at the cat. I can lecture the cat and I can plead with the cat. But no matter what I do, that cat still isn't going to bark.

If you have a relationship or any area of life that isn't working, you have a cat that isn't barking – and you are fighting it. That person is the way he or she is and that area of your life is the way that it is. This is true whether you like it or not.

When you fight the truth of the way your situation is, you destroy your effectiveness and make your situation worse. You do this in five very destructive ways:

1. You get upset and lose your ability to see clearly.

2. You destroy love and create opposition against yourself.

3. You magnify whatever you are resisting.

4. You put yourself "at the effect" and lose your power.

5. You lose your ability to see the truth.

This last item may be the most important. When you fight the truth, you destroy your ability to see the truth. When you can't see the truth, you can't see your situation for the way it really is.

When this happens, you can't see what you need to do. Handling a situation without seeing the truth is like trying to open a door when you can't see that it's locked. You may spend a lot of energy trying to force the door open, but you won't be very effective.

Once you surrender to the truth, you will be able to see your situation clearly. You may not like what you see, but at least you can see it.

Instead of trying to force open a locked door, you can put your focus on finding a key. You can take whatever action is appropriate to your situation.

The moment you surrender to the truth, you get your power back. Solutions appear and the problem area starts clearing up.

Here are some examples that demonstrate this:

Example 1

I once worked with a lady who didn't keep her word. When I asked her to do something, she would promise me that she would do it. I would then rely on her and when she didn't keep her word, I had to pay the consequences.

This went on for years. I did everything I could to get her to keep her word with me, but nothing worked. I kept relying on her and kept paying the consequences.

Finally I had a realization that changed my life. "She can't be relied on." Once I let in this truth, I could see what I needed to do. I needed to stop relying on her.

I couldn't see the truth before, because I didn't want that to be the truth. So, instead of interacting with her based on the way that she was, I interacted with her based on how I wanted her to be.

I continued to rely on her and I kept expecting her to be reliable, but she wasn't. I kept getting upset and the problem continued.

Getting upset at an unreliable person for being unreliable is like getting upset at the cat for not barking. Cats don't bark and unreliable people do unreliable things.

Once I let in the truth of her unreliability, I stopped getting upset and could see what I needed to do. I stopped relying on her. I restored my peace of mind and this area of my life ceased to be a problem.

Example 2

Maria was married to a man who drank a lot. When he drank, he would get upset and make life difficult for everyone around him. This caused all sorts of problems.

Maria did everything she could to get him to quit drinking, but nothing worked. In fact, the more she tried to get him to stop drinking, the more he drank. She didn't know what to do.

Finally, she had a realization that changed her life. She realized that he was an alcoholic and that he couldn't quit drinking even if he wanted to – and he had no interest in quitting.

She didn't want this to be the truth, but it

was the truth. He was an alcoholic and he would continue to drink no matter what she did.

When she let this in, her choices became clear. She could continue to suffer in a destructive relationship or she could get a divorce and move on with her life. She decided to move on.

Once she let in the truth, she could see the action that was needed to handle this area of her life.

Direction of focus

Look at any area of your life that isn't working and notice the direction of your focus.

Is your focus on surrendering to the truth of the way your situation is and seeing what needs to be done, or is your focus on fighting the truth?

If you look, your focus is on fighting the truth.

This is why the problem continues. Instead of focusing on solutions, the focus is on resisting. Instead of resolving the problem, it gets magnified.

To have a problem area clear up, all you have to do is change the direction of your focus.

Surrender to the truth of the way your situation is and restore your ability to see clearly. Then look to see what needs to be done and start taking action.

The moment you do this, you shift from being "at the effect" to being "at cause." You get your power back and this area of life starts clearing up.

You accomplish this through a process of healing and letting go.

Action To Take

1. At any moment, your life is exactly the way it is. The people in your life are the way they are and you are the way you are. Look at the people and the areas of life where you resist and see that this is true.

2. Notice that in every area of your life that isn't working, there is a truth that you are fighting. This area of life is the way that it is and this is true no matter how you feel about it. Notice how irrelevant your feelings are.

3. Review the five destructive ways that we sabotage our lives when we fight the truth. Then notice how they apply to the areas of your life that aren't working. Notice how fighting the truth has dramatically sabotaged your effectiveness.

4. Look at the areas of your life that don't work and notice the direction of your focus. Instead of surrendering to the truth and focusing on what needs to be done, your focus is on resisting the truth. Work with this principle until you can clearly see it in your life. This is important.

5. Notice how much more effective you would be if you could flow with whatever happens around you.

CHAPTER 8

Letting Go

Have you ever had a time when you were actively resisting something and then, for whatever reason, you stopped resisting and made peace with this area of life?

Think of a time when you did this and notice what happened. Instantly, your fear and upset disappeared. You got your peace of mind back and everything looked different.

Everything looked different because the tunnel vision was gone.

Now notice what happened to the area of life that you had been resisting. It cleared up. This is what happens when you flow with life. Life takes care of itself.

Ultimately, resisting is the only thing that keeps life from working. When you let go of the resisting, you remove the tunnel vision. You can see what you need to do and life starts working again.

You remove the resisting and subsequent tunnel vision by "letting go" of your rules for how life should be. The ability to let go is one of the most important skills you can ever learn. It's the key to creating a great life.

The moment you let go, everything seems to change. With the fear and upset gone, you become creative and able to discover solutions you could never have seen before.

To see how the process of letting go works, let's start by looking at the nature of fear.

Fear is created by resisting a future event. The more you resist the future event, the bigger your fear. The bigger your fear, the more you feel threatened. The more you feel threatened, the more you act destructively, and the more your fear comes true.

Here is an example of how this works:

Jennifer had a major fear of losing her job. The more she resisted losing her job, the more she became full of fear. This caused her to make mistakes, which put her job in jeopardy. Her fear then became stronger and she made even more mistakes. Eventually, she lost her job.

By resisting a future event, Jennifer created a process that brought her the very event that she was avoiding. This is the nature of resisting. Whatever you resist, you magnify. If she had been able to release her fear, she would have saved her job.

To have any fear lose its power, do the opposite of what creates it. Instead of resisting the future event, be willing for the future event to happen.

Now, this doesn't mean that you want the event to happen or that you will it to happen. Nor does it mean that you will stand by and allow it to happen.

Letting go is strictly a state of mind and is totally separate from your actions. Letting go is the inner technique that removes the fear, upset, and tunnel vision, so you can see what action works.

In your heart, be willing for your fear to become a reality, but in your actions, do everything you can to make sure it doesn't happen.

Whether you are resisting a future event or a present circumstance, the process for letting go is the same. Be willing for your life to be however it is and to become however it may become.

You do this by granting permission. "I am willing to lose my job." "I am willing for my spouse to leave." "I am wiling for my partner to never change." "I am willing to lose my home."

Let go of your demands for how life should be. Surrender to the truth and set yourself free inside. Then take whatever action you need to have your life be great.

To make the process of letting go a little easier, there are three very important steps you can take. The first step is to trust that you will be okay no matter what happens.

Step 1 – Trust that you will be okay.

When you know that you will be okay no matter what happens, letting go becomes relatively easy. You become more able to flow with your situation and can see what needs to be done. Life then works out fine, which makes it easier to trust.

When you don't trust, you feel threatened. You fight, resist, hang on and withdraw. This makes everything worse, which makes it harder to trust.

Whether you trust or not, is a major factor in determining the type of circumstances that show up in your life. When you trust that you will always be okay, no matter what happens, you become much more effective in your life.

Ultimately, trust is a choice. It is something that you create. You create trust by your declaration. "I will be okay no matter what happens. I trust, just because I say so."

Trust is also telling the truth. You really will be fine no matter what happens. You have had tough times before and you have gotten past every one of them. If you are in a tough time now, this too will pass.

Difficult times don't come and stay. They come and go. How fast they go depends on whether you flow with the situation or fight it. When you flow with a situation, it comes and goes quickly.

Life is only threatening when you resist. So, stop resisting and trust. Trust that no matter what happens, you will be okay.

Step 2 - Give your situation to God.

If you are engaged in your spirituality, the second step in letting go is to give your situation to God.

Let's say that I am married and have a fear of losing my wife. Here is a powerful prayer I could use:

"God, I give you my marriage and my wife. I want us to stay together, but if you have something else in mind for us, then so be it. What do you want me to do?"

It's amazing, but life always seems to clear up when you genuinely give your problems to God.

Get to the place where you are willing for anything to happen. "God, I give you my life, my heart and my soul. I give you my relationships, my prosperity and my health. I give you everything. Whatever you have in store for me is fine. I trust you totally."

When you are willing to lose everything, you cannot be threatened.

There is also something very special that happens when you let go. The items in your life don't disappear when you become willing to lose them. They are still there, but something changes in you. All of a sudden, you become very thankful for everything that you have.

If I am willing to lose my wife and she doesn't leave, how do you suppose I will feel about her? I will treasure every moment that I have with her. And the more I appreciate her, the more she will want to be with me.

The same principle applies in every aspect

of life. The more you are willing to lose something that you value, the more you will appreciate it, and the more you appreciate it, the more you will be able to keep it.

Here is another interesting point:

Our unwillingness for something to happen does not prevent it from happening. On the contrary, unwillingness dramatically increases the probability that it will happen.

The more I am unwilling to lose my wife, the more I will hang on and try to control her. My unwillingness to lose her doesn't keep her from leaving. It pushes her away.

We create unwillingness in a subconscious attempt to control life so that our hurt won't get triggered. We become unwilling for this to happen or for that to happen. We think that this will somehow protect us, but it doesn't.

Whenever there is unwillingness, there is an underlying tunnel vision that tends to bring you the very circumstances that you are avoiding.

So, be willing for anything to happen. Not in your actions, but in your heart. In your actions, do everything you can to have your dreams come true, but in your heart, be willing for your life to be however it is and however it may become.

Then watch for miracles. They will be on their way.

Step 3 – Be willing to feel your hurt.

This step is important because all our destructive behavior is done in an automatic attempt to avoid feeling our hurt.

We think that we are avoiding and resisting certain circumstances and on the surface this is true. But at a deeper level, we don't resist the circumstances. We resist all the hurt that the circumstances reactivate.

Once you are willing to feel your hurt, the need to avoid it disappears. Resisting and hanging on lose power. You become more able to flow with life and you become more able to determine how your life will be.

Action To Take

1. Find a time when you were resisting something, and then, for whatever reason, you let go of the resisting. What happened? You restored your peace of mind and this area of life cleared up. This is what happens when you let go. Find examples of this in your life.

2. Make a list of all your fears and everything in your life that you are resisting. Then go to each item on your list and notice that by your resisting, you have made your life more difficult.

3. What would your life be like if you were free of the fear, upset and tunnel vision? Notice how much happier and more effective you would be. Would you like to have this in your life?

4. Use this book to develop your ability to let go and flow with life.

5. Remember that letting go is a state of mind and is totally separate from your actions. Letting go is what allows you to see what action you need to take.

PART II

BE FREE OF THE UNDERLYING CONDITIONS THAT SABOTAGE LIFE

CHAPTER 9

Releasing Emotion

At any moment the circumstances of our lives are exactly the way that they are, and how we feel about it is totally irrelevant. So, why can't we be at peace with the truth? Why do we fight, resist, hang on and withdraw?

We fight the truth because the truth strikes a nerve. It reactivates all sorts of feelings and emotions. It's the avoidance of these feelings that gets us into trouble.

In an automatic attempt to avoid feeling our hurt, we create the fear, upset and tunnel vision that sabotages our lives.

There are basically, two types of hurt that we avoid. We avoid the emotion of our current circumstances and we avoid the suppressed hurt from our past.

Sometimes we avoid suppressed hurt from

an emotional trauma, like a rape or a beating, but this is rare compared to the childhood hurt of feeling not okay.

Whatever the hurt, the key to a major healing is the same. Get that hurt out of you.

To learn how to do this, look at little children. Little children are masters at healing hurt. When they get hurt, they cry and cry. Then, when they get through crying, the hurt is all gone.

They are able to release their emotion because they do something that we don't notice. They feel their hurt willingly. They are totally willing to feel their emotions and they don't care what anyone thinks about it.

By feeling the hurt willingly, the hurt is able to come, run its course and go. This is the natural process for healing hurt.

A good way to see this in your life is to find a time when you were hurt and you cried and cried. Then, after you cried your last tear, you felt a wonderful freedom. This will be a time when you felt your hurt willingly.

By feeling your hurt willingly, you were able to release the emotion, and the process of feeling it would have been experienced as healing.

If you took the exact same hurt and fought it, the hurt would have been experienced as pain. It would have been painful because you would have suppressed the hurt and kept it inside.

Emotional pain is not caused by your circumstances. It's not even caused by your hurt. Emotional pain exists only when you fight your hurt.

The more you fight your hurt, the stronger and more powerful it becomes. Fighting hurt is like pushing against a coil spring. The more you push against it, the more it pushes back.

So, feel your hurt willingly, like a child. Let the hurt come and let it go.

Feeling your hurt willingly becomes much easier when you realize that you don't have a choice about feeling your hurt.

When you are hurt, you are hurt. You are going to feel it whether you like it or not. Your only choice is this: you can feel your hurt willingly like a child and let it go, or you can fight it and keep it inside.

"But I feel my hurt a lot and it doesn't go away."

It doesn't go away because feeling your hurt

isn't enough to heal it. It's how you feel it that makes the difference.

The key to healing hurt quickly

There are two different ways to feel your hurt. You can either feel your hurt "at cause" or you can feel it "at the effect."

When you feel your hurt "at the effect," you are a victim of your circumstances and have no power. When you are in this state, you can cry hours a day for months and months, and have no healing.

If you take the same hurt and feel it deliberately and purposefully, "at cause," you can have a major healing in minutes.

To feel your hurt "at cause," dive into it and feel it willingly like a child. Feel your hurt because you choose to, because you want to reach in, grab it, and pull it out.

This allows the hurt to come and go quickly. This also puts you in the driver's seat. When you feel your hurt at cause, you are on top of your situation. When you feel your hurt "at the effect," you feel like your situation is on top of you.

To tell whether you are feeling your hurt "at cause" or "at the effect," notice where your focus is. If your focus is on pulling out the emotion, you are feeling your hurt "at cause." If your focus is on the circumstances, you are feeling your hurt "at the effect."

By focusing on the circumstances, you keep the hurt alive. Each time you think of the incident, you trigger more hurt. When you take your focus off of the circumstances and focus on releasing the emotion, you heal your hurt quickly.

While you are feeling your hurt, remember that emotion is nothing more than a body sensation. It's a physical reaction to a specific stimulus and is not any different than a sneeze or a yawn.

Crying is the body's way of purging negative energy and nothing more. When you suppress your hurt, you keep this negative energy from being released. You keep it inside.

So, allow yourself to feel your hurt. Feel it willingly like a child. Feel it because you want to. Let the hurt come and let it go. Then look for more.

Have you ever had a time when you ran barefoot through a field and got stickers in your feet? What do you do when this happens? You stop. You look for the stickers and then you pull them out.

It's the same with hurt. Do everything you can to find your hurt and pull it out. Pull it out because suppressed hurt profoundly sabotages your life.

The more hurt you have, the more you will be threatened by life. The more you feel threatened, the more you fight, resist, hang on and withdraw. This in turn, creates more hurt.

The more hurt suppressed you have, the more hurt you are going to get.

Suppressed hurt also has a major impact on your health. Do everything you can to get this suppressed hurt out of you. The quality of your life depends on it. Constantly look for opportunities to release more hurt.

The best time for healing is when you are in a state of fear and upset.

This is a special time for healing, because when you are in this state, your hurt has just been triggered and brought to the surface. When your hurt is on the surface, it's relatively easy to reach in, grab it, and pull it out.

The first step in releasing your hurt is to separate your circumstances from the emotion.

To do this, notice where the circumstances

are located. Are they outside of you or are they inside? Obviously, they are outside of you. Now notice where the emotion is located. It's inside of you.

The circumstances and the emotion seem to be connected, but they're not. They are totally separate. As long as you think that they are connected, the circumstances will have total power over you. You will remain "at the effect" and you will have little or no healing.

The moment you separate the circumstances from the emotion, the circumstances lose their power, and you get your power back.

After you make the separation, the next step is to get the emotion out of you. This restores both your peace of mind and your effectiveness.

To release the emotion, dive into your hurt and cry it as hard as you can. Feel the hurt deliberately and purposefully. Feel the hurt of your circumstances and the deeper hurt of feeling worthless, not good enough, or whatever your hurt is.

If there is not enough emotion to cry like a child, fake it. Faking the tears coupled with an exaggeration of the emotion can be just as effective as actually crying.

To do this, physically exaggerate the feelings. Get into the emotion as much as you can and put a lot of energy into it. Literally fake the tears.

When you exaggerate the emotion, you are doing the opposite of fighting it. You are putting it there. This puts the healing process into high gear.

Learning how to release emotion without crying is very important. This is because most of the time when we have fear or upset, there are no tears.

The more you release your emotion, the more you will be able to flow with life, and the better your life will be.

In the next chapter, you are going to learn how to be free of the childhood hurt that is so destructive.

The avoidance of this deeper hurt creates the core issues that are responsible for all the self-sabotaging behavior in our lives. Finding and healing this deeper hurt is one of the most important things you can ever do for yourself.

Action To Take

1. On the surface, we resist certain circumstances, but on a deeper level, we don't resist the circumstances. We resist all the emotion that the circumstances reactivate. Look in your life and see that this is true

2. Get your list of fears and the aspects of your life that you resist. Then go to each item on your list and notice the feelings and emotion that you don't want to feel. Notice how much you avoid feeling this hurt.

3. Now notice that you don't have a choice about whether you are going to feel this hurt. You will. Your only choice is to feel it willingly like a child and let it go, or feel it unwillingly and keep in inside.

4. Find a time when you were hurt and you cried and cried. Then, after you cried your last tear, you felt a wonderful freedom. This is a time when you felt your hurt willingly. Notice how much better you felt once you were free of the emotion.

5. Go through life looking for opportunities to release more hurt. Whenever you get upset, dive into the emotion. Feel it deliberately and purposefully. Fake the crying if you need to. Let the emotion come and let it go.

CHAPTER 10

Healing Core Issues

Every one of us has several core issues that totally run our lives. Each of these issues are created by the automatic, subconscious avoidance of a very specific hurt from the past.

The hurt that we avoid is the childhood hurt of feeling worthless, not worth loving, not good enough, or some other form of feeling "not okay."

This hurt varies from person to person and each person avoids it in a different way. But the result is always the same: any area of life where this hurt manifests will be a disaster zone.

This area of life will be full of fear, upset, and tunnel vision. We will fight, resist, hang on and withdraw. We won't be able to see clearly and we will act in a way that creates opposition and resistance against ourselves.

Every area of life that doesn't work can be traced to the automatic, subconscious avoidance of this hurt. This includes all of our suffering and all of our self-sabotaging behavior patterns.

Finding and healing these core issues is one of the most important things you can ever do. Until you heal this hurt, you will be forced to repeat the past, and you will keep attracting more of the very hurt you are trying to avoid.

Fortunately, this is a hurt that can be healed. You take away much of its power and you can heal a major part of it very quickly. You can heal it quickly because the hurt isn't based on fact; it's based on thoughts.

Do you remember the little girl who got yelled at for being stupid? To say that the little girl really is stupid is nonsense. Being stupid has nothing to do with the truth. But it has everything to do with her hurt.

The same thing is true for whatever your hurt is. To say that you are worthless or not good enough could never be the truth.

In fact, as we will soon see, it is physically impossible for you to be worthy or worthless, good enough or not good enough. It is impossible because these are only thoughts and opinions. They do not exist in the physical universe.

They only exist in our mind.

You can search the whole world over for a *good enough*, but you will never find one. If you found one, what color would it be and how much would it weigh?

Can you go to the store and buy a pound of *worthy* or a bottle of *success*? No. You can't, because *worthy* and *success* are not things. They are thoughts.

Worthless has never caused you any trouble. All the trouble has been caused by the actions you have taken to avoid feeling this way. It's the fighting, resisting, hanging on and withdrawing that has sabotaged your life.

Worthless has never caused you any trouble because *worthless* doesn't exist. It is just a thought. It's the fighting of this thought that creates all the suffering.

We spend our whole lives running from something that doesn't even exist.

Although judgment does not exist in reality, it's very real in our reality. In the realm of thoughts, we are both worthy and worthless, good enough and not good enough, loveable and unlovable. We are everything.

One moment we'll feel one way and in the next moment we'll feel another way. These are all aspects of being human. They are in each of us.

The problem comes when there are aspects of ourselves that we are not at peace with. When this happens, we run from them, and we create a state of tunnel vision that takes away our power and sabotages our lives.

For example, most people are at peace with the aspect of themselves called coward. If you are one of these people, this area of your life will work effortlessly.

If you are fighting this aspect of you, your life will be very different. To prove you are not a coward, you will constantly be putting yourself in dangerous situations. Coward will frequently be "in your face," and this area of your life will be a mess.

If you made peace with this aspect of you, the tunnel vision would disappear. The destructive behavior would stop and this area of life would clear up.

Coward does not show up in the lives of people who are at peace with this aspect of themselves. It only shows up in the lives of people who are fighting it. If you are fighting coward, coward will keep showing up in your life, over and over.

The same is true for any aspect of you that you are not at peace with. If you are running from *failure*, life will keep bringing you *failure*. If you are running from *unlovable*, life will keep bringing you *unlovable*.

Fighting these aspects does not make them go away. It magnifies them in your life

Do you remember the example of the yellow balloons? The more you fight the balloons, the more yellow balloons you get. It is the same with *worthless, not good enough,* or whatever your issue is.

Judgment is nothing more than a thought, and like the yellow balloons, the more you fight the thought, the stronger it becomes. Everything you do to get rid of *worthless* creates more *worthless.*

To heal this hurt, you need to do the opposite of what gives it power. Instead of fighting these aspects of you, make peace with them. Own them and embrace them.

Get to the place where you can say, "Yes. I am totally worthless. So what? I am also totally worthy. These are both aspects of me." When this happens, the issue loses power and disappears.

Example

Most of my life was spent running from failure. This was an aspect of myself that I did not want to face. In an automatic, subconscious attempt to avoid feeling this hurt, I created a core issue that sabotaged my life.

In my drive to become a success, I would overspend and take unreasonable financial risks. I created a life of fear, upset, and tunnel vision. I lost my ability to see clearly and acted in a way that produced more and more failure.

Finally, I failed so completely, I was forced to face this aspect of myself. I lost everything. I lost my investments, my office, and even my home. Failure was "in my face" like never before.

As I looked over my life, I couldn't help but see what a failure I was. The evidence was overwhelming.

I was forced to let in what I had feared the most. I didn't like what I saw, but I could no longer avoid it or deny it. Success was also an aspect of me, but at the time, all I could see was failure.

As I let in this aspect of myself, and as I allowed myself to feel the hurt of being this way, something very special happened. My fear of failure lost its power.

Once I saw, deep in my soul, what a failure I was, I could no longer fight it. It's like running from your shadow. You can't. When I couldn't fight this aspect of me, there was nothing to give it power.

It's like the yellow balloons. When you stop fighting them and let them be there, they disappear. Once I stopped fighting failure, it lost its relevance and disappeared.

I was sad for a while, but soon my whole outlook changed. The fear and upset that ran my life was no longer there. I no longer had to be a success. I could just be me. This was an incredible relief.

I hadn't been able to be me since I was four years old. I thought that in order to be okay, I had to be a success. I never dreamed that this was just something I had made up. I never dreamed that it was okay to just be me.

This new freedom produced a very subtle, yet profound change in the way I lived my life. Instead of running from failure, I was able to put my focus on having my dreams come true and creating a life that works

Up to this point, I couldn't see what worked. In fact, what worked was irrelevant. "Don't bother me with what works. I'm not interested. Tell me how to avoid failure. I'm interested in that."

By running from failure, I lost my effectiveness, sabotaged my dreams, and created more failure. Once I made peace with this aspect of myself, there was nothing to fear. The tunnel vision disappeared and both success and failure lost their power.

With the tunnel vision gone, I could put my focus on creating a life that works. I stopped overspending and I got out of debt.

I continued to go for my dreams, but I did so in a way that was effective. As time went on, my dreams began to come true. Now I have a life that I could never have imagined.

My life turned around the day I made peace with failure. The same thing can happen for you. You can be free of the hurt that sabotages your life.

Fortunately, you don't have to do it the hard way. You can walk through the healing process using this book.

Action To Take

1. What is the childhood hurt that runs your life? Are you worthless, not worth loving, a failure, or not good enough? Notice that avoiding this hurt does not make it go away. Avoiding this hurt makes it grow stronger.

2. Notice the fear, upset, and tunnel vision that has been created by the automatic avoidance of this hurt. Any area of your life that isn't working is an area where this tunnel vision is present.

3. Fortunately, this is a hurt that can be healed. You can heal it because the hurt isn't based on fact. It's something that you made up as a child. See if you can find a *worthless* or a *not good enough*. Notice that you can't.

4. *Worthless* and *not good enough* have never caused you any harm. All the harm has been caused by the resisting and hanging on. It's the avoidance of your hurt that has sabotaged your life. Look at your life and see that this is true.

5. Notice how different your life would be if all of this hurt were gone. Notice the freedom you would have if you could say, "Yes, this is an aspect of me. So what? I'm also the opposite."

CHAPTER 11

Find the Hurt

The first step in the healing process is to discover, as specifically as possible, what the hurt is. Ultimately, this hurt, or core issue, will be some form of feeling "not okay."

It's not the truth that you are this way. It's just an old, suppressed, childhood emotion. It's the avoidance of this emotion that sabotages your life.

To find this hurt, look for the words of "not okay" that are the most uncomfortable. Are you worthless, not good enough, not worth loving, or a failure? The more painful the words, the closer you are to your hurt.

While you are looking, pay special attention to any words of "not okay" that you deny being. "I know I'm not a failure. I don't feel that way at all. I'm a success."

As you will soon see, *worthy* and *worthless, success* and *failure,* are all two sides of the same coin. If you can see one side of the coin but not the other, you have found a major hurt.

To see if this really is a hurt that you are avoiding, notice how painful it would be if this were true about you. If this is painful, you have found a hurt that runs your life.

Remember, you are not looking for the truth. You are looking for the hurt. The truth and the hurt are never connected. They are in two different realms. To find your hurt, look for it on an emotional level, not an intellectual level.

For most people the bottom line hurt is *worthless* and of *no value.* Other common core issues include *not worth loving, failure, not good enough,* you are *just like your parents,* and *stupid.*

Since the primary hurt for most people is *worthless,* I will use that word throughout the book as a general reference to all core issues.

While you are looking for your hurt, you may find lots of words that are painful, but for now, look for the ones that hurt the most. Be as specific as possible.

To describe your hurt more accurately, you may

want to use a combination of words. Consider combinations like these: *worthless failure, hopelessly unlovable, stupid loser,* or *weak, whiny wimp.*

Use the following sections to find your hurt.

How is your relationship with your parents?

Your relationship with your parents is one of the best places to look for your hurt. This is especially true if your relationship with one or both of your parents was painful.

To find your hurt, go back in time and put yourself in the hurt that you experienced as a child. Then answer this question, "According to the hurt, what incredibly painful thing would it say about you if your own parents treated you this way?"

Would it say that you are worthless, not worth loving, or not good enough? Look for the words that hurt the most.

Then notice how you would feel if your parents were right about you – that you really are this way. How would you feel if your parents were totally justified in their actions because you are so worthless or whatever your issue is?

If these are fighting words, if this would be

very painful, or if you are quick to deny it, you have probably found your primary hurt.

What are your upsets?

Every time you have been upset, some core issue has just been triggered. By looking at the times you have been upset, you can discover what your hurt is.

Make a list of all the times you have been hurt and all the times you have been angry. List every major upset that you have had in your life. See if you can come up with at least twelve incidents. The longer your list, the easier it will be to find your hurt.

After your list is complete, go to each incident and put yourself in the hurt of what happened. Then look to see what those circumstances say about you. Remember, don't look for the truth. Look for the hurt.

If someone left you, this could say that you are unlovable or not worth loving. If you got fired from your job, this could say that you are not good enough or a failure. Find the words that are the most uncomfortable.

As you work with your list of upsets, you will discover that the same words keep showing up. Make a note of these words and look for more.

Once you think you have found your hurt, ask yourself, "If I really am this way, what would this say about me?" Use this question to see if there is a hurt that is even deeper than the one you have found.

What are your fears?

Make a list of all your fears. Then, for each fear, find the hurt that you would have to feel if your fear came true. What would those circumstances say about you? Put yourself in the emotion and find the words that are the most painful.

What do you need for your happiness?

The key word here is "need," which is very different from desire. Desire can give you the power to have your dreams come true. "Need" will push your dreams away. It's the "need" that gets us into trouble.

In reality, we don't need anything for our happiness because happiness can only come from within. The feeling of need comes from avoiding a very specific hurt.

For example, if you need a loving, supportive relationship for your happiness, you are probably running from *unlovable* or *not worth loving*. If you need wealth, you are probably running from *failure* or *not good enough*.

To find your hurt, identify what you "need" for your happiness. Then look for the opposite. What hurt would you have to feel if you could never get what you want? What would those circumstances say about you?

A similar way to find this hurt is to look for what you are driven towards. This is because we are never driven towards something. We are always driven from something. There is a hurt that we are avoiding.

If you are driven to be a success, you are running from failure. If you are driven to be strong, you are running from *weak*. If you are driven to be right, you are running from being wrong, and more specifically, *stupid*.

Find what you are driven toward and look for the opposite. Then notice how painful it would be if you really were this way. The more painful this is, the closer you are to your hurt.

What are the areas of your life that don't work?

Any area of life that doesn't work is an area where you are resisting. You are resisting this area of life because it triggers a hurt.

If you suffer in the area of relationships, you may be running from *not worth loving*. If your finances are a mess, you may be running from *failure* or *not good enough.*

List the main areas of your life that don't work. Where do you suffer? Then find the hurt that you are avoiding. According to the hurt, what do these areas of life say about you?

Has rejection or abandonment been an issue for you?

Would an incredibly wonderful person be rejected or abandoned? No. Not according to the hurt. So, what kind of person would this happen to?

What would it say about you if you were rejected or abandoned? For most people, this would say that you were worthless and either unlovable or not worth loving. Notice how painful it would be if this were true about you.

What do you resist in your parents?

How would you feel if you were exactly like your parents? For most people, this is a very uncomfortable thought. Notice if this is uncomfortable for you.

If you resist certain aspects of your parents, you will resist these aspects wherever they show up. You will resist them in other people and you will resist them in yourself.

What are the aspects of your parents that you resist? List every one of them. Each one will be an aspect of you that you are fighting.

You may not do the same things that your parents do, but this doesn't mean that the aspects aren't in you. Notice how much you strive to be the opposite. You wouldn't strive to be the opposite unless you were running from something.

Ironically, the more you resist being like your parents, the more you become exactly like them. Once you see that you are just like your parents, that quality stops growing in you, and your resistance towards your parents gets replaced with compassion.

A list of common core issues

Look over the following list of common core issues and make a list of the words that reactivate the most hurt.

If possible, have someone read the words to you. Hearing a word is much more reactivating than reading one. Listen to each word as though it accurately describes the very essence of you. Notice the words that are particularly painful.

How would it feel if you really are:

unlovable

undesirable

not worth loving

not good enough
  to be loved

not worth respecting

don't have what it
  takes to be loved

worthless

have no value

have deficit value

flawed

no good

not good enough

inadequate

inferior

less than

useless

a nothing

insignificant

unimportant

don't count

don't matter

disposable

a throwaway

a nobody

a loser

a failure

underachiever

don't measure up

can't cut it

don't have what it takes

incompetent

screwed up

something is wrong
  with you

can't do anything right

stupid

unstable

defective

not acceptable

weak

a coward

irresponsible

unreliable

lazy

self-centered

inconsiderate

selfish

dishonest

bad

wrong

evil

repulsive

heartless

a horrible person

ugly

fat

a slut

just like your parents

your parents were
  right about you

What is your core issue?

Now go back and read this chapter again. See if any new words stand out. Then select the word or words that most accurately describe your hurt.

By now, you have probably found many words that are painful. For example, you may have the hurt of *worthless* and also the hurt of *failure, stupid* and *not worth loving.* Select the words that hurt the most.

You can work with all of your core issues later, but for now, find the ones that are the most painful.

If you feel stuck, or if you have difficulty finding or healing a core issue, call our office and schedule a telephone consulting session. This is a great way to get to the other side of an issue. Our phone number is (713) 520-5370.

Once you find the words that most accurately describe your hurt, you are ready for the next step.

Action To Take

1. Use this chapter to find the hurt that runs your life. Look for the words that most accurately describe the emotion that you are avoiding. Be as specific as possible.

2. Remember, you are not looking for the truth, you are looking for the emotion. So don't look to see if you are a certain way. Instead, notice how you would feel if this were true about you. The more painful this would be, the closer you are to your hurt.

3. While you are looking, pay special attention to any words of "not okay" that you deny being. "I know I'm not worthless. I don't feel that way at all." If you deny being a certain way, you have probably found a major hurt.

4. Be sure and review the list of common core issues. If possible, have someone read them to you. Hearing an issue is more reactivating than reading one.

5. Review this chapter several times. Then select the words of "not okay" that are the most painful. Write them down.

CHAPTER 12

The Illusion of Judgment

After you discover the aspects of you that you have been resisting, the next step in the healing process is to make peace with them.

"But I don't want to make peace with them. I want to get rid of them."

Well, you can't. You can't because they are not objects; they are thoughts. And like the yellow balloons, everything you do to get rid of them gives them more power.

You cannot get rid of these aspects, but you can make peace with them. You can get to the place where you can say, "Yes, I am this way. So what? I'm also the opposite."

This takes away both their relevance and their power. But you can't just jump to "so what?" It may be true that judgment is an illusion and has no power, but knowing this on an intellectual level doesn't change a thing.

When you know this deep in your heart, on an emotional level, it changes your life. You get this awareness by facing this part of you.

These core issues are like a dragon that chases us through life. Once you stop running from the dragon and face it, you discover, on a profound, emotional level, that the dragon is an illusion and has no teeth.

Instantly, both the dragon and the tunnel vision lose power. You see life clearly. Solutions appear and the problem areas of your life start clearing up.

Facing the dragon may not sound like much fun, but once you discover the illusion of judgment, the healing process becomes relatively easy.

No judgment is real.

Worthless feels threatening because we think it's real. We think that there really is a thing called *worthless* and there really is a thing called *worthy*, but this is an illusion.

Worthless and all the other words of judgment can only exist as opinions. They can never exist in reality. They can only exist in the eyes of the beholder.

Look at the chair you are sitting on. Is it good enough? One person would say, "Yes. Of course it is." Another person would say, "No it's not. It's the wrong size and the wrong color. I don't want it."

Two people have totally different opinions about the same chair. One person says that it's good enough. The other person says it's not. So, what is the truth about the chair? Is it good enough or not?

The truth is neither. The chair is just the chair and nothing more. Any judgment we have about the chair is something we add to the truth.

Now notice where the judgment is located. Is it in the chair or is it in the eye of the beholder. Obviously, it's in eye of the beholder.

You can judge the chair as being one way or the other, but your judgment will never be more than a point of view. It may be a valid point of view, depending on your perspective, but it will never be the truth.

Is the chair strong or is it weak? It's neither. It's just the chair. However, if you compare it to a locomotive, the chair would be considered weak. If you compare it to a feather, the chair would be considered strong.

In a limited comparison, you could say that the chair is one way or another, and this would be a valid point of view. But if you take away the comparison, the point of view would no longer be valid.

To say that the nature of the chair is strong or weak, good enough or not good enough, can never be the truth. The chair is just the chair and nothing more.

Consequences, however, are very real. Everything you do or don't do will have a consequence. Our judgment about the consequences is something that we make up.

Let's say that I get fired from a job. There are very real consequences to getting fired. My judgment about it will just be an opinion.

Are you a success or are you a failure? If you compare yourself to a homeless person, you could consider yourself to be a success. If you compare yourself to a financial tycoon, you could consider yourself to be a failure.

If you had the Hope diamond, which is worth millions of dollars, and put it beside a glass of water, which would be more valuable?

If you were dying of thirst in the desert, the water would be considered more valuable. If you were given plenty of water and placed in a jewelry store, your point of view would quickly change.

No matter what point of view you have about something, someone else will have a very different opinion about the same thing. Your point of view is just one way of looking at something. It is not the truth.

Take a moment and look at your judgments about people and life. Notice that with each judgment, someone else could have a very different opinion about the same thing.

See if you can find a judgment that is the truth. If you are honest, you won't be able to. Judgments are never more than opinions.

Notice that it would be physically impossible for you, or anyone else, to be *worthless*. You could judge yourself as being this way, but never, under any circumstances, could this be the truth.

Now look at the other side of the coin. Notice that it would also be physically impossible for you, or anyone else, to be *worthy*.

This is often harder to see because we want there to be a *worthy*. We want *worthy* to be real because this is our hope of escaping *worthless*.

But like all judgments, *worthy* and *worthless* can only exist in our mind.

Worthy and *worthless, good enough* and *not good enough, success* and *failure, lovable* and *unlovable* are all just judgments. They are never the truth.

Work with this concept until you can see that no judgment is ever the truth. This is very important, so take some time and do it now.

Two sides of the same coin

Judgment cannot exist as a thing. It can only exist as a thought, and in the realm of thoughts, there is a very particular way in which judgment must show up. Judgment must show up in a package of opposites.

A good way to see this is to imagine a ladder leaning against your house. If you have *up* the ladder, you must also have *down* the ladder. *Up* and *down* must come together in the same package.

You can never have *up* without having *down* because *up* can only exist if you have *down* to compare it to. If there is no *down*, there can be no *up*.

Up and *down* are two sides of the same coin.

You either have both sides of the coin or no coin at all. Never will you have only one side of the coin. *Up* without *down* cannot exist.

The same is true for all judgment. *Worthy* cannot exist unless you have *worthless* to compare it to. *Success* cannot exist without *failure*. *Lovable* cannot exist without *unlovable*.

Judgment can only exist as a mental concept consisting of two opposite points of view. This mental concept then becomes the standard by which we judge ourselves and others.

The standards we use to judge

People who run from stupid go through life judging themselves and others by the standard of *smart* and *stupid*. People who run from failure judge by the standard of *success* and *failure*.

You can tell what someone's core issues are by listening to the words of judgment that person uses. If someone frequently uses the words *success* and *failure*, that person is running from failure.

The standards we use to judge are the result of our hurt.

For example, if you don't have the hurt of *coward*, you won't be able to judge in terms of brave and coward. If there is no hurt, the words will have no relevance.

Do you remember the little girl who got yelled at? The moment she decided that she was stupid, she created the mental concept of *smart* and *stupid.* Since this is her hurt, *smart* and *stupid* will seem very relevant.

She will then go through life judging herself and others by this standard. One moment she will judge herself as being smart. In the next moment, something will happen and she will judge herself as being stupid.

She will never notice that she is judging. She will think that she is observing the absolute truth of the universe, but she's not. She is judging.

Find a time when you judged yourself or someone else as being a certain way. Didn't your judgment appear to be the absolute truth? Notice how real your judgment seemed. Now notice that this wasn't the truth. It was just your judgment.

Judgments seem to be the truth, but they are not. They are just thoughts, but they are thoughts that totally run our lives.

Work with this chapter until it becomes obvious that we spend our lives running from something that doesn't even exist.

Action To Take

1. See if you can find a judgment that is the truth of the universe. Notice that you can't. No matter what point of view you have about something, someone else will view the same thing in a very different way.

2. Notice that it is physically impossible for you or anyone else to be either worthy or worthless. These are just points of view. Work with this concept until it becomes very clear that no judgment can ever be the truth.

3. Judgment can only exist as a mental concept consisting of two opposite points of view. *Worthy* and *worthless* are two sides of the same coin. Notice that you can never have one side of the coin without also having the other.

4. Neither side of the coin exists in reality, but both sides are very real in your reality. One moment you feel one way, and in the next moment, you feel another way. Notice how real both sides of the coin are to you.

5. When you judge yourself or another person as being a certain way, doesn't your judgment seem to be the truth? It does, but notice how impossible it would be for this to actually be the truth. No matter how real a judgment may seem, it can never be more than an opinion.

CHAPTER 13

Facing the Dragon

Years ago I worked with a man who was running from failure. In his drive to be a success, there was a point where he purchased a million-dollar home. He was so proud of himself because he had finally become a great success.

Then one afternoon, he went for a drive and discovered that his house was the smallest house in the entire neighborhood. Instantly, he was devastated. He had become a worthless failure, once again.

One moment he was a great success. A moment later, he was a worthless failure. What happened? Did he change from one moment to the next? No.

He was the same man before and after after he went for his drive. Nothing changed except his point of view. He just went from one side of the coin to the other.

In reality, it would be physically impossible for him to be either a success or a failure, but in his reality, he is both. One moment he feels like a success. In the next moment he feels like a failure.

The same is true for you. It would be physically impossible for you to be worthy, worthless, a success, a failure, or whatever your core issue is. These are only thoughts.

However, in your reality, you have a very different story. In your reality, each side of the coin is very real. One moment you feel one way, and in the next moment, you feel the other way. You are both sides of the same coin.

The nature of each side of the coin

Whichever side of the coin you are on, the feeling will be total. You will never feel half worthy and half worthless. You will only experience yourself as being one way or the other.

When you are on the side of the coin called *worthy*, it's like looking through blue-tinted sunglasses. Everything you see takes on the color of *worthy*. Your very essence is worthy. You always have been and you always will be.

When you look at your life from this side of the coin, there will be an overwhelming amount of evidence to prove how truly worthy you are. It will appear to be the absolute truth of the universe.

Then something will happen and you will get upset. Instantly, you move to the other side of the coin and look at your life through the orange-tinted sunglasses called *worthless.*

When you are on that side of the coin, you are totally, permanently, hopelessly, forever, worthless or whatever your core issue is. You always have been and you always will be.

This is the essence of the dragon. You are totally, permanently this way. There is no blue anywhere. And if you look at your life from this side of the coin, there will be a ton of evidence to prove it.

We don't run from the hurt of feeling partially worthless. We run from the hurt of feeling totally worthless. We run from the "truth" that the very core of our being is worthless, not good enough, or whatever our core issue is. We really are this way.

This is the essence of our hurt, and if you look at the times when you were in the very depths of your hurt, this is the hurt you felt.

Notice how incredibly painful it would be if

this were true about you. You really are totally, permanently, this way. Notice that you would do almost anything to avoid feeling this hurt.

This is the hurt that creates the tunnel vision and sabotages your life. Healing this hurt is probably the single most important thing you can ever do.

You heal this hurt by doing the opposite of what gives it power. You give this hurt power by avoiding and resisting it. You take away its power by owning and embracing it.

The process of owning and embracing the dragon is relatively easy once you know it's just an illusion, but to heal this hurt, you still need to face it.

When you face the dragon, it is important to treat your hurt as though this is the absolute truth of the universe about you. You really are this way.

This is important because down deep, on an emotional level, this is the truth. It's the truth of your universe. It was placed there as a little child. You have just been fighting it.

Now it's time to own this part of you and get your power back.

Five elements of facing the dragon:

1. Find the specific hurt that runs your life.

Find the words of not okay that are the most painful. You can work with all the words later, but for now, select the ones that hurt the most.

2. See all the evidence to prove that this is an aspect of you.

Put yourself in the hurt of the side of the coin that you are avoiding. Then, from that hurt, look over your life, on an emotional level, and see all the evidence to prove that you really are this way. There will be plenty of evidence if you are willing to see it.

3. Let in the "truth" that you are this way.

This is the opposite of fighting it. The more you let in the "truth" that you are this way, the more impossible it is to fight it. When you can't fight it, the hurt loses power and disappears.

4. Feel the hurt willingly like a child.

We avoid these aspects of ourselves because we don't want to feel the hurt. So, dive into the hurt and feel it willingly like a child. Feel it deliberately and purposefully because you want to reach in, grab it, and pull it out.

5. Move to the place of "so what?"

As you face the dragon and allow yourself to feel the hurt of being this way, you automatically move to the place of "so what?" The dragon loses power and you set yourself free.

The next chapter will walk you through the process of facing the dragon and healing your hurt.

Action To Take

1. Put yourself on the side of the coin called worthy and see all the evidence to prove how truly worthy you are. You always have been worthy and you always will be. Let this in.

2. Now put yourself on the side of the coin called worthless and see all the evidence to prove how totally worthless you are. This is also the truth about you. You always have been this way and you always will be.

3. Notice that whichever side of the coin you are on, it appears to be the absolute truth of the universe. Work with this until you can see that both sides of the coin are very real in your reality and that each side appears to be the truth.

4. Notice how much you have avoided the "truth" that you really are totally worthless or whatever your core issue is. Look at the times in your life when you were in the depths of your hurt and notice that this is the hurt that you felt. This is the hurt that needs to be healed.

5. You heal this hurt by doing the opposite of what gives it power. Instead of avoiding and resisting it, own it and embrace it. Review the elements of facing the dragon and get ready to set yourself free.

CHAPTER 14

The Healing Process

Now it's time to start the healing process. You have a unique opportunity to be free of the hurt that has been sabotaging your life. You can have a freedom and a peace of mind that you haven't experienced in years.

The process for healing your hurt and setting yourself free is relatively easy, but it takes some diligence.

Reading the chapters and understanding the process won't be enough to change your life. To change your life, you need to experience the healing deep inside.

You do this by walking through the healing process on an emotional level, rather than an intellectual level.

Recall the specific hurt that you are going to work with and dive into it. Allow yourself to feel all the hurt of being worthless, not worth loving, not good enough, a failure, or whatever your core issue is.

Put yourself in the emotion. Then use the following questions to heal your hurt. The more you are in touch with your hurt, the easier it will be to heal it.

Work with each question until you can say "yes" and mean it. Take your time and allow yourself to experience the truth of each answer. Let in the hurt and look for evidence to prove that you really are this way.

Now it's time to begin. Put yourself in the hurt and walk through the following questions:

• Notice the years and years of hurt associated with being this way. Isn't this a hurt that you would do almost anything to avoid feeling?

• Do you see the enormous amount of energy and effort that you have spent avoiding this hurt?

• No matter what you have done to avoid this hurt, doesn't this hurt keep showing up in your life, over and over again?

• Notice that the more you have avoided this hurt, the more you have had to experience it.

Do you see that this is true?

- Would you like to heal this hurt?

- Are you willing to face the dragon?

- Are you willing to stop fighting this hurt?

- Are you willing to feel *all* the hurt of being this way?

- Are you willing to feel this hurt, willingly like a child, and let it come and let it go?

Notice that you don't have a choice about whether you are going to feel this hurt or not. You will. Your only choice is this: Are you going to feel it willingly, like a child, and let it go, or are you going to fight it and keep it inside?

Create within yourself a desire to look for more of this hurt so you can find and heal more of it.

- Can you see a lifetime of incidents where you have felt this hurt?

- Hasn't every incident been more proof that, down deep, you really are this way?

- Are you willing to discover that this is true about you?

- Can you look over your life and see a lifetime of evidence to prove it? Let this in.

This is the most important part of the healing process. To the extent you know that this really is an aspect of you, it becomes impossible to run from it. The core issue loses power and your hurt disappears.

Put yourself into the hurt of feeling this way and look over your life. Search for all the evidence to prove that you are this way. Look at all the times you have been upset and all the times you have felt the hurt of being this way. Each incident will be more proof.

Let in the "truth" that you are this way and allow yourself to feel your hurt. Get to the place where you can see the evidence everywhere you look.

Take a few moments now and let in how incredibly worthless, etc., that you really are. Let this in. The more you let this in, the more you heal your hurt. Do this now. Let the hurt come and let it go.

- Now that you look, isn't this an aspect of you? It's there isn't it?

- Notice how irrelevant your feelings are. Even if you hate it and deny that this aspect exists, isn't it still there? Isn't this still an aspect of you? Let this in.

- Would it be accurate to say that you have spent most of your life avoiding it and trying to make it go away?

- Do you see how much you have suffered and sabotaged your life in the process?

- Do you see that by your resisting this aspect of you, you have only made it stronger?

- Are you now willing to stop fighting this aspect of you? Are you willing to make peace with it?

- Do you now give this aspect of you full permission to be in your life?

Notice that once again, you don't have a choice. This aspect of you is going to be there whether you like it or not. You can either fight it and give it more power, or you can make peace with it and have it lose power.

- Are you willing to surrender to the truth of its existence?

- Do you now give this aspect of you full permission to be in your life and to never, ever, go away?

- Are you willing to be this way?

- Are you willing to be this way forever and to never change?

- Are you willing to be this way forever and still have a wonderful, love-filled life?

We think that our worthlessness and other aspects will keep us from having a great life, but they don't. In fact, it's the opposite. These issues are the key to a great life.

As you own these aspects of you, the ego loses power. You become an expression of love and life starts working for you instead of against you.

So, welcome your worthlessness and all the other aspects of you that you have been avoiding. Allow yourself to be human and set yourself free.

- Do you see that most of your life has been spent running from this aspect of you, doing everything you can to become the opposite?

- Now that you look, do you see how much you have suffered and how much you have sabotaged your life trying to be a certain way?

- Isn't it true that no matter how hard you have

worked to become a certain way, you haven't gotten there yet?

* Do you see that you never can?

It's impossible. Trying to have *worthy* without *worthless* is like chasing a rainbow. You can never get there, but you can certainly create a lot of suffering in the attempt.

* Do you see the enormous pressure you have put on yourself, having to be a certain way?

* Can you imagine the incredible freedom and relief you would have if you never had to be a certain way?

* Would you like to have this freedom?

* Are you willing to give up having to be a certain way? Are you willing to give it up forever, and just be you?

* Can you give yourself permission to be human?

Do you feel a difference inside? Do you feel more freedom and peace? Do you feel more able to be yourself?

As you accept the "truth" that you really are this way and discover that being this way is truly, "so what?", you experience a wonderful peace. The dragon loses power and you become free.

Keep working with this until you feel this freedom. Get to the place where you can say, "Oh, how wonderful. I'm worthless. What a relief. Now I don't have to prove I'm worthy. I can just be me."

Take the time to do this exercise with all the words that you have found to be painful.

If you are fighting the "truth" that you are this way, you are avoiding your hurt. To get past the denial, notice that no matter how much you fight this side of the coin, it's still there. Notice that your feelings about it are totally irrelevant.

So, create the desire to feel your hurt. Do this so you can be free of it.

Resisting this aspect of you doesn't make it go away. It is still an aspect of you. You don't have to like it, just surrender to the truth of it and allow yourself to feel the emotion.

Remember that this is not the only aspect of you. This is just one of thousands. You are also the opposite. You are also an incredibly wonderful person.

Keep in mind that being a certain way doesn't

mean a thing. "I am this way. So what? I'm also the opposite. What does this have to do with tomorrow? Absolutely nothing. I can still do what works and I can still have a great life."

Action To Take

1. Use the questions in this chapter to make peace with all the aspects of you that you have been resisting. Start with the issues that are the most painful. Work with each question until you can say "yes" and mean it.

2. Make sure you walk through the healing process on an emotional level rather than on an intellectual level. This is important because the hurt is in the emotion, not the intellect.

3. Do everything you can to see that you really are this way. Let in the hurt and look for all the evidence to prove that this is true about you. You really are this way. The more you let this in, the more impossible it is to run from it, and the more the hurt loses power.

4. While you are letting in the hurt, gently move to the place where you can say, "Yes, I am this way. So what." Get to the place where you experience the freedom of no longer having to be a certain way.

5. Notice the relief that comes from facing the dragon. Notice how freeing it is to just be you. Allow yourself to be human.

CHAPTER 15

Steps For More Healing

How does it feel now to be worthless, not good enough or whatever your core issue is? Do you feel a new freedom? Do you feel more at peace? Do you feel more able to be yourself?

Once you face the dragon and discover that it is just an illusion and has no teeth, it permanently loses power. It will still be there, and it may still chase after you, but it ceases to be a threat.

Eventually, you can get to a point where you are so at peace with the dragon that it literally disappears from your life. For example, if you are at peace with the aspect of you called *coward, coward* won't show up in your life.

If you are resisting *coward* or any other aspect of yourself, these aspects will keep showing up in your life, over and over. They keep showing up so you can make peace with them.

To say this another way, life will bring you an unlimited number of opportunities for healing. These opportunities will arrive most often in the form of fear and upset. Your job is to use these opportunities for all the healing you can get.

Whenever you find yourself in a state of fear or upset, use the following steps to restore your peace of mind and heal more of your hurt.

Steps to take when you get upset

1. Whenever you get upset, go to the moment the upset began and find the specific circumstance that you are resisting. What happened? Be as specific as possible. If you are in a state of fear, find the specific circumstance that you are avoiding.

2. Separate the circumstances from the emotion. Notice that the circumstances are outside of you. The emotion is inside. They are not connected in reality, only in your mind.

3. Dive into the emotion and feel the hurt of your circumstances. Feel the hurt deliberately and willingly like a child. If there aren't any tears, fake the tears. Exaggerate the emotion. Let the hurt come and let it go.

4. While you are in the emotion of your circumstances, look for the deeper hurt. What

do those circumstances say about you? Find the aspects of you that you are avoiding and dive into the hurt of being that way. Feel the hurt willingly like a child.

5. Look over your life and see all the evidence to prove that you really are this way. See the evidence and let it in. The more you let this in, the more the hurt loses power.

6. Gently move to the place of "so what?" Remember that you are also the opposite. You are also a wonderful person. Give yourself permission to be human.

7. After you restore your peace of mind, look to see what, if any, action you need to take. Then take it.

When you go through life looking for more hurt, it becomes harder and harder to find it. It becomes harder because there is less hurt to find.

Be free of past hurt.

Make a list of every incident from your past that still has emotion associated with it. If a particular incident triggers emotion, write it down.

Then work with each incident to find and heal more hurt. Use the same steps that you would use to release an upset.

Put yourself in the hurt of what happened. Then go back in time and walk through the event. Dive into the emotion and feel it deliberately and purposefully. Feel the hurt of the circumstances and the deeper hurt of your core issue.

The purpose of this exercise is to release all the suppressed emotion from your past that you are aware of. Make sure you do this with every incident on your list. Keep doing this until all the suppressed emotion is gone.

Then make a list of your fears and use the same process to heal more hurt.

With each fear, imagine that your fear has come true. Then dive into the emotion and feel it willingly like a child. Let the hurt come and let it go. Keep doing this until all the emotion is gone and you are willing for each of your fears to come true.

Remember that willingness is a state of mind and is totally separate from your actions. By being willing for your fears to come true, you greatly decrease the chance that they will.

Do everything you can to get this hurt out of you. The more you heal your hurt, the less life will need to bring it to you.

Keep a log of your upsets.

Go through life looking for opportunities for more healing. One way to do this is to keep a log of your upsets.

Every time you get upset, write it down. You don't need a lot of details, just enough to remind you of the incident. Then look for the core issues that are being triggered. What do those circumstances say about you?

Sometimes you will find the hurt quickly. Sometimes it takes longer, but keep looking. At first, you will work with the obvious core issues. Then, as time goes on, you will discover new issues and deeper levels of old ones.

By keeping a log of your upsets, you force yourself to look at your issues.

As you continue to work with these issues, your upsets become noticeably less frequent and less severe. You soon reach a point where you rarely become upset.

Do you want to keep your hurt?

Do you have any resistance to letting go of your hurt? Usually, there is a part of us that doesn't want to let go of our core issues. If this is true for you, you are certainly not alone.

So, why would we want to hang on to something that causes so much pain and suffering? We hang on to our hurt because it's the perfect excuse.

As long as we have our hurt, we don't have to be responsible for our lives. "What can you expect of me? I'm just worthless. I don't have to risk anything. I don't have to take action. I don't have to be responsible. I can blame others for my life. I can be a victim".

Notice if you have used your hurt as an excuse in life. If you have, notice how this excuse has held you back, taken away your power, and kept you from taking action.

Now notice if you have an explanation or story surrounding your hurt. This happened and that happened. Your parents caused this and your circumstances caused that.

Blaming our past is another subconscious tool we use to avoid taking responsibility for our lives. "What can you expect of me? I have this horrible past. I'm wounded. I can't do great things. I can't determine what will happen in my life."

When you believe that your life is the way that it is because of your past, you limit what you can do about your future.

Take a look now and decide if you are willing to give up both your hurt and the story surrounding it. Are you willing to give up being able to use either your hurt or your story as an excuse for anything? Are you willing to take full responsibility for what happens in your life?

Keep working with this until you no longer need either the story or the hurt.

Get with a friend.

Here is an exercise that will take healing even deeper.

Get with a friend and tell the person all the aspects of you that you have been resisting. Then give the person all the evidence to prove that you really are this way. Be specific and give details.

This exercise is important because if you can't talk about your issues, you can't own them. If you can't own them, you can't heal them.

Telling someone of your worthlessness is like communicating an upset and getting it off your chest. When you do this, the upset loses power. The same thing happens when you talk about your worthlessness.

While you are revealing these aspects of you,

be light about it. Joke about it and be playful. The more you can laugh about your issues, the more insignificant they become. This exercise can be very healing.

Then tell your friend all the aspects of you that you are proud of. What are your gifts and talents? What are your accomplishments? What are all the qualities of you that you consider to be valuable?

This part of the exercise is important because if you can't talk about your greatness, you can't own it. If you can't own your greatness, you can't express it.

To get a head start with these exercises, get a pad of paper. Then write down all the evidence to prove that you really are worthless, not good enough, or whatever your core issues are. Spend some time on this. Write down everything you can think of.

While you are making your list, let in the "truth" that you really are this way and allow yourself to feel all the hurt. Use this exercise for all the healing you can get.

After you finish your list, and have fully let in the hurt of being this way, tear up the list and throw it away. Then start a new list.

This time, write down all the evidence to prove how truly great you are. Write down everything you can think of and feel the joy of being this way. After your list is complete, tear it up and throw it away.

Then do the exercise again. Do it several times. Each time you do the exercise, your core issues lose more power.

This is a very important exercise. Make sure you do it even if you don't do the exercise where you get with a friend.

The more you can stand on either side of the coin, the more the coin loses relevance and disappears from your life.

As you own both your worthlessness and your greatness, you become whole and complete. You cannot be threatened and you cannot be hurt.

Instead of avoiding fear, you can put your focus on creating a life of love and having your dreams come true.

Allow yourself to be human.

We have been taught that in order to be loved, we have to be worthy, successful or good enough. This is what we have been taught, but it's totally opposite of the truth.

You never love someone because you judge the person as being worthy, successful or good enough. You may respect the person for being this way, but you won't love the person. That person certainly won't melt your heart.

You get your heart melted when someone allows him or herself to be human, when someone sheds a tear or is willing to be vulnerable. This is what melts your heart.

In our weekend workshop, *Return To The Heart*, people discover this in a profound way. As we watch people own the aspects that they have been running from, two things happen:

First, you see very clearly that the hurt has nothing to do with the truth. You wonder how the person came up with his or her issue. "Worthless, that's nonsense." "Not good enough? Where did you come up with that?"

Second, you fall in love with the person. As the person owns his or her hurt, that person becomes very human and melts your heart. You feel safe. You feel loved and you become much more able to be yourself.

The same thing happens when you own your worthlessness. Your ego stands aside. You become very human and you create the experience of love.

It may seem uncomfortable to be human, but this is the key to having more love than you have ever had in your life. It's also the key to having your dreams come true.

As you allow yourself to be human, you tap into a power much greater than you. You become an expression of love. You light up the world and life works for you instead of against you.

Life is so much easier when you allow yourself to be human.

Action To Take

1. Use the exercises in this chapter to heal all the hurt you can find. Then go through life looking for more. Every time you face more of the dragon, more of it disappears. Every time you feel more of your hurt, because you want to, more of it goes away.

2. Is there part of you that wants to keep your hurt? For most of us, there is. We want our hurt so we don't have to be responsible for our lives. We can blame and hold back. Look now and see if you are wiling to permanently give up being able to use your hurt as an excuse for anything.

3. Make a list of every incident from your past where you still have suppressed hurt. Then use the steps in this chapter to release all the emotion. Get to the point where there is no incident from your past that has any power over you today. Then do the same thing with your fears.

4. Allow yourself to be human. We put so much pressure on ourselves trying to be a certain way. Are you now willing to give this up? Are you willing to be human? Are you willing to just be you? This is the key to having your dreams come true.

CHAPTER 16

The Opportunity of Life

In most of our workshops, we do an exercise where participants create a cycle of loving, supporting, and empowering each other. The result is a profound state of oneness.

People experience a connection with each other and with life that is beyond words. Upsets and problems disappear. All that exists is a deep state of love, freedom, and inner peace.

Then we look at the nature of this state. People discover that, in this state, the circumstances of life have no power. Fear and upset cannot exist. Judgment disappears and the past has no relevance. Even the ego and the concept "me" disappear. All that exists is love.

When you live in this state, you are happy, alive, and free. You can flow with whatever happens. You are confident, creative, and very effective. You radiate a very positive energy, solutions appear, and great things happen around you.

This is the state where miracles are common. This is also the natural state. It's the essence of who you are. This is what you experience when you are free of the baggage of your past.

The only thing that keeps us from experiencing this state is our inability to flow with life. To avoid feeling our hurt, we fight, resist, hang on and withdraw. This in turn destroys love and sabotages our lives.

As you heal your hurt and develop your ability to flow with whatever happens, the destructive behavior fades away and something very special shows up in its place: you become very appreciative.

When you are willing for anything to happen, you automatically become thankful for everything you have.

This state of appreciation then creates a feeling of abundance, which creates more abundance. As you appreciate life, life appreciates you.

It's the same principle that applies when you appreciate another person. That person automatically appreciates you in return.

As you appreciate life, you radiate a very positive energy. Life then opens its doors and starts giving you its treasures. Healing your hurt and developing your ability to flow with life allows this to happen.

The process for accomplishing this is relatively simple, but it doesn't happen by itself. You have to take action. Make healing your hurt a top priority. It's one of the most important things you can ever do.

Use this book to learn how. Read it over and over. Every time you read it, you discover something new. You take the healing a little deeper and you become more effective in your life.

If you want to learn more about how to create a life that works, read my other books, *Miracles Are Guaranteed* and *How To Heal a Painful Relationship*. You can also attend our workshops and do the *Mastery of Life Audio Course*.

Life is too short to have it be anything less than wonderful.

Thank you, and
I love you.

Bill Ferguson

Additional Support

The *Mastery of Life Audio Course* is an easy way to make a profound change in your life. This course walks you through the process of healing your hurt, changing the way you live your life, and creating a life that works for you instead of against you.

If you want individual support, call us at (713) 520-5370. Our telephone consulting sessions can be life-changing. We also invite you to attend our weekend workshop, *Return To The Heart*.

You can get more information at:

www.billferguson.com
www.masteryoflife.com

We look forward to hearing from you.

Return To The Heart[SM]
A weekend workshop

If you have a relationship or any area of life that isn't working, there will always be an underlying condition of resting or hanging on that is creating the problem. Until this underlying condition is removed, you will be forced to repeat the past.

This weekend workshop is about discovering and healing this underlying condition. It's about opening your heart, healing, and making a permanent change in the way you live your life.

The awareness you gain will restore the very essence of who you are. The result is more love and a greater ability to flow with life. You will be noticeably more creative and far more effective.

Participants say that it is physically impossible to live life the same way after you *Return To The Heart.*

Friday: 7-10:30 P.M.
Saturday: 10 A.M. to 10 P.M.
Location: Houston, TX
Cost: $375
$275 for each additional participant

For dates and more information, visit:
www.billferguson.com
www.masteryoflife.com
or call 713-520-5370

MASTERY OF LIFE AUDIO COURSE

A Step-By-Step Process For Having Life Work.

10 Audio CDs with Workbook

This life changing course is about creating miracles. It is about learning, healing, taking action, and developing the skills you need to transform your life.

You will walk though the process of healing the inner issues that sabotage your life. Then you will learn how to create a life where miracles become common.

Topics include love, healing, restoring peace of mind, cleaning up your life, relationships, prosperity, life purpose, spirituality, and more. This powerful course provides an awareness and a healing that will literally change your life.

ISBN 1-878410-43-1   Ten Audio CDs & Workbook............ $135

MIRACLES ARE GUARANTEED

A HANDBOOK FOR LIVING

A Step-By-Step Guide To Restoring Love, Being Free, And Creating A Life That Works.

This book is also available on 2 Audio CDs

Paperback, 136 pages

Similar to the *Mastery of Life Audio Course*, this profound yet simple book shows, step-by-step, how to create a life where miracles show up. You will learn how to flow with life and create a life of love. You will discover how to take charge of your life, find your life purpose, and experience your spirituality. This handbook for living provides a powerful roadmap for having life work and is a great supplement to the audio course.

ISBN 1-878410-38-5 Paperback.............................. $15

ISBN 1-878410-39-3 Two CDs $22

HOW TO HEAL A PAINFUL RELATIONSHIP

And If Necessary, To Part As Friends

This book is also available on 2 Audio CDs

Paperback, 156 pages

In this unique book, Bill Ferguson shows, step-by-step, how to remove conflict and restore love in any relationship. You will learn what creates love and what destroys it. You will discover how to end the cycle of conflict, heal hurt, release resentment and restore your peace of mind. Bill's experience as a former divorce attorney provides rare insight into the nature of relationships. You will discover something about yourself and your relationships that will change your life forever.

ISBN 1-878410-25-3 Paperback.. $15
ISBN 1-878410-31-8 Two CDs $22

GET YOUR POWER BACK

Find And Remove The Underlying Conditions That Destroy Love And Sabotage Your Life.

This book is also available on 2 Audio CDs

Paperback, 131 pages

Whenever a relationship or any other area of life isn't working, there will always be an internal, underlying condition that is creating the problem. This hidden condition takes away your power, keeps you from seeing what needs to be done, and makes your situation worse. Until you find and remove this condition you will be forced to repeat the past. Once you remove this condition, this area of life clears up. This incredibly, profound book walks you through the process of finding and removing this condition. The result is more love, more effectiveness, and a much more enjoyable life.

ISBN 1-878410-41-5 Paperback.. $15
ISBN 1-878410-42-3 Two CDs $22

THE INCREDIBLE POSSIBILITY OF LIFE

Join Two Brothers Sharing a Profound Wisdom That Will Change Your Life

1 DVD

Running Time: 136 minutes

In this powerful video presentation, Bill and his brother Randy share life-altering insights and healthy doses of brotherly ribbing that will move you, challenge you, and make you laugh. You will discover a truth that awakens a potential you didn't know you had. You will discover practical ways to restore love, joy, vitality, balance and effectiveness in your life. Be ready to laugh, have fun, and change your life.

ISBN 1-878410-40-7   One DVD $30

BOOKS & CDs

ITEM		PRICE	QTY.	AMOUNT
Mastery of Life Audio Course 10 CDs & workbook		$135		
Miracles Are Guaranteed	Paperback	$15		
	2 CDs	$22		
How To Heal A Painful Relationship	Paperback	$15		
	2 CDs	$22		
Get Your Power Back	Paperback	$15		
	2 CDs	$22		
Incredible Possibility of Life	DVD	$30		

Subtotal	
Texas residents add 8% sales tax	
Shipping and Handling:	$6.00
Plus 10% of Subtotal	
Total	

Name (Please print): _____

Address: _____

City: _____ State: _____ Zip: _____

Telephone: Day: _____ Eve: _____

For Credit Card Orders:

Card No.: _____ Total $: _____

Exp. Date: _____ Signature: _____

To order by mail, send your check or money order to:
Return To The Heart, P.O. Box 541813, Houston, TX 77254

For telephone orders, call:
713-520-5370 or fax to 713-523-8412

To order online or to download any of our products, visit:
www.masteryoflife.com

If you want to have a telephone consulting session with Bill Ferguson or a member of his staff, call us at (713) 520-5370.

You can find us on the internet at:
www.billferguson.com
www.masteryoflife.com